5-MINUTE STORIES FOR FEARLESS GIRLS

5-MINUTE STORIES FOR FEARLESS GIRLS

Sarah Howden
Illustrations by Nick Craine

Collins

5-Minute Stories for Fearless Girls
Text copyright © 2018 by HarperCollins Publishers Ltd.
Illustrations copyright © 2018 by Nick Craine.
All rights reserved.

Published by Collins, an imprint of HarperCollins Publishers Ltd

5-Minute Stories for Fearless Girls includes certain imagined elements in tales based on real events.

HarperCollins books may be purchased for educational, business,
or sales promotional use through our Special Markets Department.

HarperCollins Publishers Ltd
2 Bloor Street East, 20th Floor
Toronto, Ontario, Canada
M4W 1A8

www.harpercollins.ca

Library and Archives Canada Cataloguing in Publication
information is available upon request.

Lettering design on pages 1, 15, 29, 43, 57, 71, 85, 99, 113, 127, 141, and 155 by Lola Landekic

ISBN 978-1-44345-536-7

Printed and bound in China
19 20 SCP 10 9 8 7 6 5 4 3

Contents

FLYING HIGH

You could say Amelia Earhart was destined to fly.

When Amelia was seven, she and her friends built a roller coaster in her backyard. They worked all day on the sloping wooden track until finally it was finished.

"I want to go, Millie!" said her little sister, Pidge.

"It's better that I try it first," Amelia explained. "I don't want you to get hurt."

3

She grabbed the cart they'd made from a wooden box and some old stroller wheels and climbed the ladder to the roof of the tool shed. Settling in, she looked out at the faces of her friends, watching below.

"Here goes!" she said, and she gave herself a push.

The cart rolled swiftly down the ramp, and for a brief moment, Amelia soared.

Then—**WHAMMO**—she and the cart slammed into
the ground. The cart skidded off in one direction
and Amelia rolled and bounced in another, bumping
and scraping to a stop.

Her friends raced over to help her up and check if she was okay. She looked a sight, bruised and dirty, her dress torn.

"Your lip is swelling!" Pidge said, her eyes filling with tears.

But Amelia looked at her sister and grinned. "Oh, Pidge," she said. "It's just like flying!"

Twenty-eight years later, Amelia was grown up.
But she wasn't all that different. She still loved to fly.

It was seven o'clock on May 20, 1932, when she climbed into the cockpit
of her bright-red plane—the one she called her "Little Red Bus"—ready for
the long flight ahead.

If she made it, she would be the first female pilot ever to fly across the
Atlantic Ocean alone.

The fuel tanks were full and she had her usual snacks at her side: a can
of tomato juice and some chocolate. It was time to go.

She steered the plane down the runway and took off into the sky. It was a
clear night, and at first, all seemed well as her plane coasted over the sea.

Until—**CRASH! BOOM!** A thunderstorm tossed her little plane around as rain pelted down. Then, worse, the rain turned to ice. Ice was dangerous. Ice could damage her instruments, make the plane stall. Amelia had to quickly dive lower to try to warm up the plane and melt the ice.

If she flew too low, she'd end up in the ocean. But if she went too high, she would be back in the storm . . .

The only choice left was the middle, where the fog was as thick as marshmallow. Even though she could barely see, she told herself to just keep going. A pilot has to keep calm, even when things get rough.

It was exhausting, but Amelia made it through to morning, when the weather settled. But now the plane was low on fuel and it was starting to shake and shudder. She had to land—fast.

Nearby, in Londonderry, Ireland, cows were grazing in a pasture beside a farmhouse when—**ROOOAARR**—Amelia's plane swooped in and chugged and clattered to a landing.

A farmhand ran over to greet the pilot . . . and was amazed to see a woman climb out of the cockpit.

"Have you flown far?" he asked.

"From America," Amelia replied.

To him, she seemed quite calm, as if she'd just been for
a short drive. But inside, Amelia was buzzing with pride.

I've done it! she thought. *I've really done it.*

She was the first woman, and the
second person ever, to fly nonstop across
the Atlantic Ocean. It took her fifteen hours.
And it all started with that spunky little girl
on the homemade roller coaster, willing
to try anything.

MISTY ON STAGE

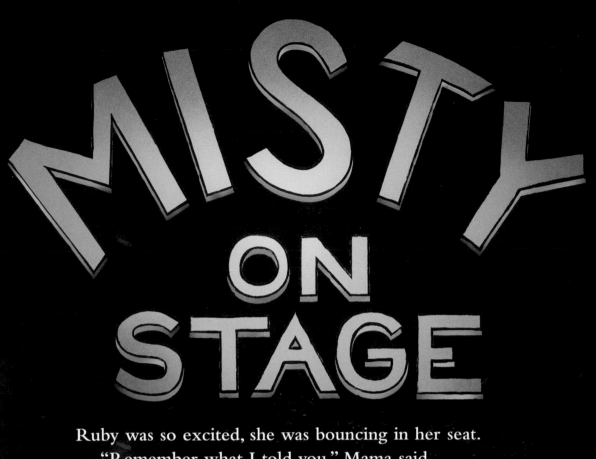

Ruby was so excited, she was bouncing in her seat.

"Remember what I told you," Mama said.

"No talking, no fidgeting, just watch the ballet," Ruby said, nodding. Then she stood up and did a little twirl—a pirouette, it was called in ballet—because she couldn't help herself.

"Show-off," muttered her sister, Jasmine, who was two years older and acted like she was bored by everything.

This was the best Christmas present Ruby had ever gotten. She'd been taking ballet classes for three years now, but she'd never seen a real live ballet. And now here they were, at *The Nutcracker*!

But the reason Ruby was most excited was she was going to see her idol, Misty Copeland, perform.

"Did you know Misty Copeland started dancing when she was thirteen?!" Ruby told Jasmine.

"So?" Jasmine said.

"That's old!" said Ruby.
"Well, it's not exactly *old*," Mama cut in.

"But most ballet dancers actually start training much younger than that—when they're three or four," she explained. "So it's pretty impressive that Misty picked it up so late."

"Oh," Jasmine said. She had quit ballet years ago. Ruby didn't understand that at all.

"Misty was so good, her teacher gave her lessons for free!" Ruby continued, smoothing down the skirt of her tutu.

Ruby wanted to be a ballerina when she grew up, even though her friend Emily had told her she couldn't. When Ruby had asked why, Emily said, "Your legs are too short," and strutted away, nose in the air.

19

"Even though she was a great dancer, *some* people thought Misty didn't have the right body for ballet. Because she's so strong," Ruby said, flexing her arm muscles. "But Misty proved them wrong."

Mama nodded as she flipped through the program, but she wasn't really listening. She'd heard all these stories from Ruby before.

"Also, she's the first-ever African-American principal dancer in the American Ballet Theatre!" Ruby told Jasmine. "Principal dancer means star dancer," she whispered, in case Jasmine didn't know.

This time, Jasmine actually seemed interested. "Really?" she said.

Just then, the lights dimmed and the chatter that had filled the huge space died down. Finally, the curtains opened.

It was a lit-up fairytale world up there. Like TV, except better: Ruby felt as if she could touch it. In their fancy costumes, the dancers were like dolls, twirling and gliding. Ruby didn't think it could get any better—and then Misty appeared, playing the Princess.

She was stunning in her gauzy white dress, floating across the stage on her toes as if it were the easiest thing in the world. When the Prince lifted Misty up above his head, she looked like she was flying.

"She's like a fairy," Ruby whispered to Mama, who smiled and said, "Shhh."

Every time Misty danced, the crowd would
clap and cheer, and Ruby would too. Ruby
imagined herself up there one day, twirling
and dipping and leaping.

When the show ended,
the crowd was on its feet,
applauding while the dancers
took their bows. They cheered
loudest for Misty, yelling,
"Brava, brava!"

24

Could it really be over already? Ruby didn't want to go home yet. Mama must have read her mind because she said, "Let's go get a milk shake."

25

Once they were sitting in the bright light of the diner down the street, drinking their strawberry shakes, Mama asked, "So? What did you think?"

26

"It was the best!" Ruby gushed. "And Misty was so amazing."

"She really was," Jasmine said. Ruby blinked: Had Jasmine just agreed with her? "Must have been hard, being the only black person in all her classes . . ." she added quietly.

"I'm sure it was, honey," Mama said with a sigh. "But one thing's for certain: She's opening the door for plenty more. Isn't that right, Ruby?" She gave her a wink.

Ruby grinned back, and
they all sat for a minute,
drinking their milk shakes.
    "Mama?" Jasmine blurted.
"Can I start taking ballet
again?"

RUTH WAKEFIELD, ONE SMART COOKIE

Imagine a world where there are no chocolate chip cookies.

It's a dark and gloomy place, isn't it?

What would you eat with a glass of milk? Or when you're sneaking a snack before bed? Okay, there are other choices: crackers, apple slices, a piece of pie . . . but none of these are the same.

Nothing fits in your hand quite the same way as a chocolate chip cookie, or has that combination of buttery, crunchy, chewy goodness, with the melty chunks of chocolate hidden inside.

But here's the thing: There was a time not that long ago when the chocolate chip cookie didn't exist. It's true.

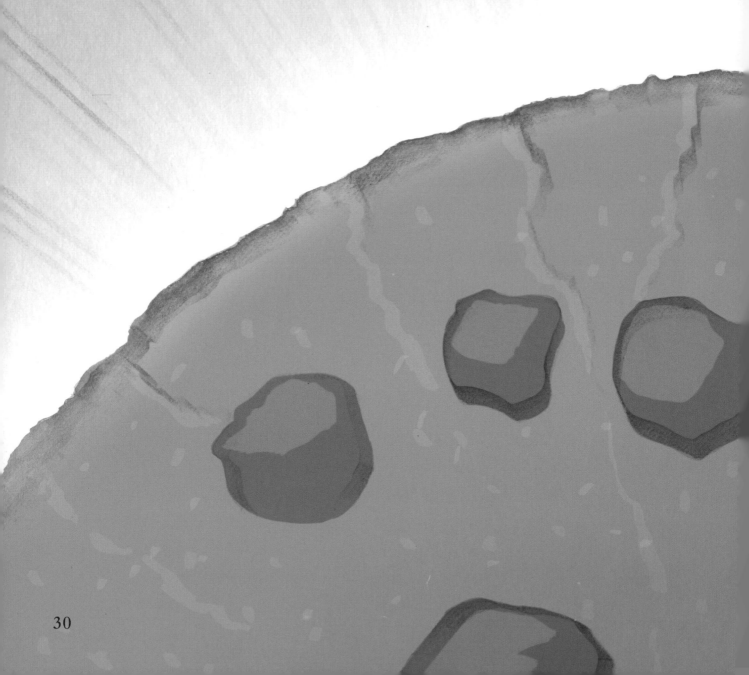

It took a special person to bring this glorious goody into the world so that the rest of us would never have to do without—and her name was Ruth Graves Wakefield.

Back in the 1930s, Ruth and her husband, Ken, owned the Toll House Inn near Boston, Massachusetts. Ruth was a great cook, and the Toll House restaurant quickly became famous for her delicious lobster dinners and tasty desserts, like Boston cream pie, brownies, gingerbreads, and puddings.

Not only that, but when customers were waiting to order, their table got a basket of fresh pecan rolls to quiet any grumbling tummies. Yum!

TOLL HOUSE - WHITMAN, MASSACHUSETTS

But the origin of the chocolate chip cookie was humble—it all started with some little butterscotch cookies Ruth used to serve on the side of a dish of ice cream. They were just extras, add-ons to the main event.

Until she started thinking:
How can I make these a little more delicious . . .

Over the years, people have said the chocolate chip cookie was invented by mistake—that while Ruth was making some butterscotch cookies, she ran out of nuts and put in chocolate on a whim, or that she accidentally knocked some chocolate into her dough while she was mixing.

But the truth is better. This wasn't an accident. Ruth was a talented woman and a fantastic cook. No, she spent time dreaming this up. The chocolate chip cookie was baked in her imagination long before she made the first batch. She was a cookie genius.

And so one fateful day, Ruth added some chopped-up chocolate chunks to the butterscotch cookie dough and baked up something magnificent—she called them chocolate crunch cookies.

Right away, they were a hit at the restaurant. So she added the recipe to her cookbook, *Toll House Tried and True Recipes*.

Word got around that these cookies were life-changing, so more and more people started baking their own at home.

During the Second World War, many Massachusetts families started sending the cookies in care packages to soldiers who were fighting far away. These men shared with their friends, and soon soldiers from all over the United States were asking for chocolate chip cookies!

Back when Ruth was baking, there was no such thing as a "chocolate chip." Instead, Ruth's recipe called for a semi-sweet Nestlé chocolate bar, cut up into little pieces. Stores could hardly keep Nestlé chocolate bars on the shelves.

And this is when Ruth had another top-notch idea. She offered Nestlé a deal—they could print her recipe on the back of their chocolate bars, in exchange for one dollar . . . and **A LIFETIME SUPPLY OF CHOCOLATE**.

Nestlé agreed, and soon everyone who bought the company's chocolate had Ruth's recipe at hand.

Even better, Nestlé created the chocolate chip (or as they call them, "chocolate morsels") just so people could make cookies without all the chopping.

People argue to this day about what makes the perfect chocolate chip cookie, but there's no arguing that Ruth's recipe is still one of the best—even after nearly ninety years.

Do you like your chocolate chip cookies crunchy or soft? With nuts or without? Bigger than your hand or bite-sized? No matter how you prefer them, the next time you bite into one, think of Ruth Wakefield: the brilliant baker who made our lives so much sweeter.

THE WOMAN WHO ROARS

The woman walks onstage and introduces herself. Her speaking voice is soft and sweet, her words peppered with giggles.

And then, she begins to sing.

Right in front of you, she transforms. Prowling the floor like a cat, she growls and sighs and roars, stretching her voice like it's made of Plasticine. Her breath comes in a rhythm you can feel in your bones.

The sounds she makes seem to come from everywhere, painting images of so many things: the howling of a wolf, the changing shapes of the clouds in the sky, the churning of a motor.

With her song, she takes you on a journey through unknown worlds, transports you across landscapes.

She tells a story without words.
Who is this? you wonder.

This is Tanya Tagaq.

She has always been creative, but Tanya didn't start making music until she moved away from home, when she was nineteen.

She grew up in the small town of Cambridge Bay, Nunavut, an Inuit community above the Arctic Circle. The land there is vast and beautiful, with a huge sky and no trees. Because the ground is mostly sea ice, there are no roads either—you have to take a plane to get there.

The natural world is very much a part of living up North, and Tanya loved to go wandering for hours, exploring and listening to the sounds around her.

And then she moved
to Halifax, Nova Scotia,
for art school.

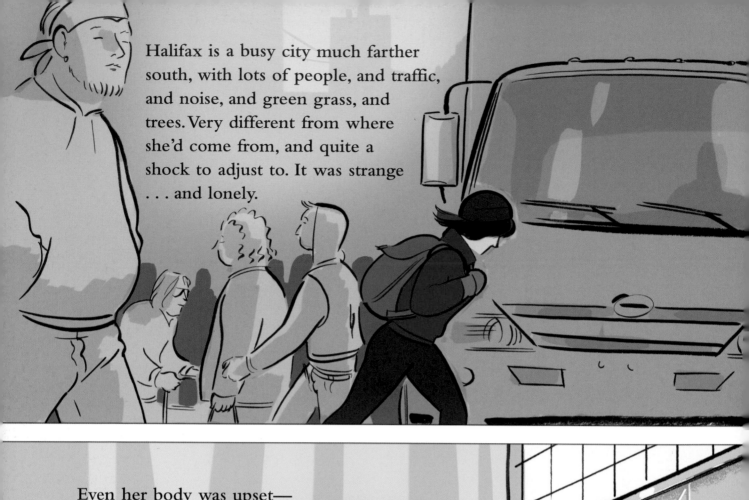

Halifax is a busy city much farther south, with lots of people, and traffic, and noise, and green grass, and trees. Very different from where she'd come from, and quite a shock to adjust to. It was strange . . . and lonely.

Even her body was upset— her lungs hurt from all the car exhaust.

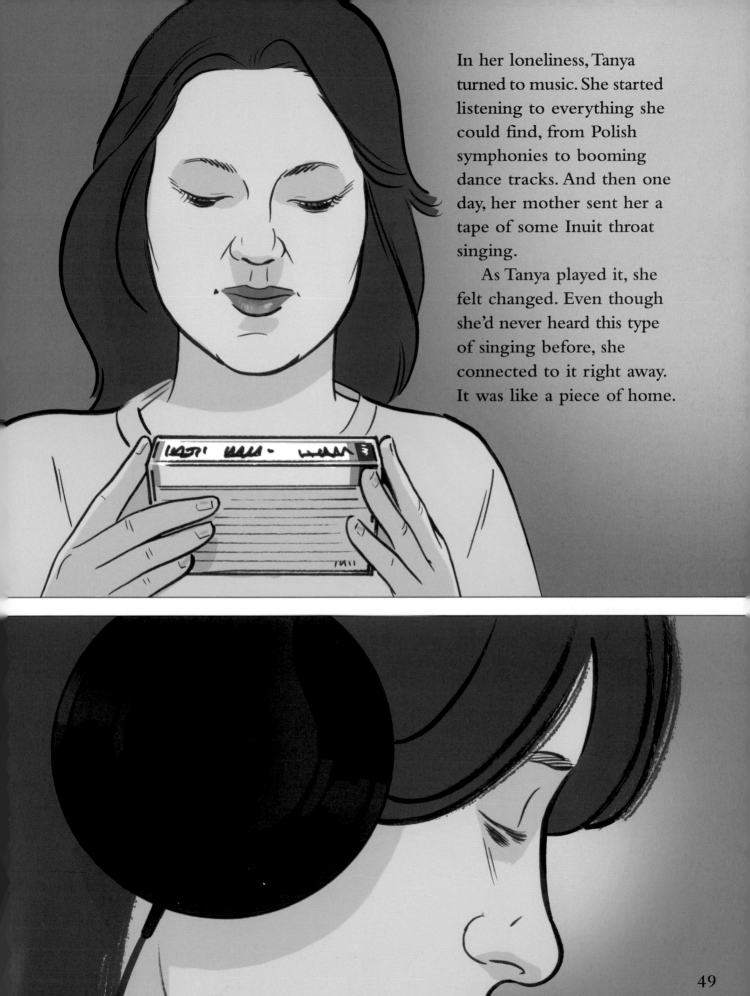

In her loneliness, Tanya turned to music. She started listening to everything she could find, from Polish symphonies to booming dance tracks. And then one day, her mother sent her a tape of some Inuit throat singing.

As Tanya played it, she felt changed. Even though she'd never heard this type of singing before, she connected to it right away. It was like a piece of home.

49

Women in the Inuit culture, Tanya's culture, have been practicing throat singing for thousands of years.

Traditionally, throat singing is performed as a playful game between two women. They stand facing each other and call back and forth, using their throats and breath as instruments, mimicking the sounds of nature. They get a rhythm going and see who breaks first—or who starts laughing.

Tanya could feel her people's history in this music, and she knew she wanted to learn more.

But since she was in Halifax, far from the Inuit people who could have taught her, she decided to teach herself. And she'd have to keep the rhythm all by herself too—there was no one else to sing with.

51

She practiced in the shower, trying to find those parts of her voice she had never used. Over and over again, she would work with her throat to make these new sounds. Once she found them, they felt so natural.

52

If you ask Tanya how to learn throat singing, she will say to try to sound like your dog. Keep working on that for about a year, and you'll be halfway there.

   That's what she was doing—untraining her voice from what she was used to and learning to use it in a different way. Finding a voice that was deeper inside herself.

Like a mix of her Cambridge Bay roots and her Halifax art school years, Tanya's music mingles her style of throat singing with pop and punk music. The result is something fierce, vibrant, and new.

She uses her music to speak out about things that trouble her, from the need to take care of the earth to the mistreatment of Indigenous Peoples in Canada. And the world is listening. Because what she's saying matters. And because the way she's saying it is powerful and astonishing.

Even when others don't understand her sound, Tanya doesn't let that stop her. She's making music that comes from her heart. It's new and it's old, and it's her very own.

VIOLA DESMOND TAKES HER SEAT

Viola Desmond's face has been on a Canadian stamp, and she is on the nation's new $10 bill.

Her hometown of Halifax, Nova Scotia, named its new ferry after her, and Montreal has a street called Rue Viola-Desmond.

But back in 1946 she was just a woman sitting alone in a jail cell thinking, *How did I get here?*

Even though it was the middle of the night, she sat up straight and tall on the dirty cot. She couldn't sleep. It was too strange, too bright, too frightening.

She knew one thing, though:

She wasn't going to cry. Not here. So she kept herself busy—she got out a pen and pad and made a to-do list.

After all, she owned her own beauty school and salon . . . people depended on her. She couldn't just go to pieces.

Looking down at her beautiful dress and her elegant white gloves, she still couldn't believe this had all started with a trip to the movies.

There she had been, stuck in the small town of New Glasgow for the evening after her car had broken down.

But Viola, as always, had stayed calm about it. No use getting upset about changed plans. She'd just make the most of her night off.

So she wandered down to the Roseland Theatre, with its twinkling lights, and bought a ticket to see a movie.

Back then, you had to choose between
a downstairs seat and the balcony. The
downstairs ticket cost more, but you could
see better. Viola had bad eyesight, so she always
sat downstairs—where she sat that night.

But she'd barely had a moment to get comfortable before an usher tapped her shoulder. "Ma'am, I believe you have a balcony ticket."

Sure enough, when she checked, there it was: BALCONY, clear as day. How did he know?

Back out at the ticket booth, Viola said, "I'd like a downstairs ticket, please."

As she spoke, she saw a cloud pass across the cashier's face.

"We don't sell downstairs tickets to you people," the woman said.

A chill spread through Viola.

She understood now. What the cashier was saying was because she was black, she had to sit in the balcony. Only white people could sit downstairs.

This racism wasn't new to Viola. It was very familiar. She had seen a lot of it over the years and always tried to rise above it. Now here she was, a businesswoman who had made a good name for herself, and she was still getting treated this way.

Viola was normally a quiet person who tried to make the best of things. But at this moment, it became too much. Too much of being treated like the dirt under people's feet.

She took her ticket back and

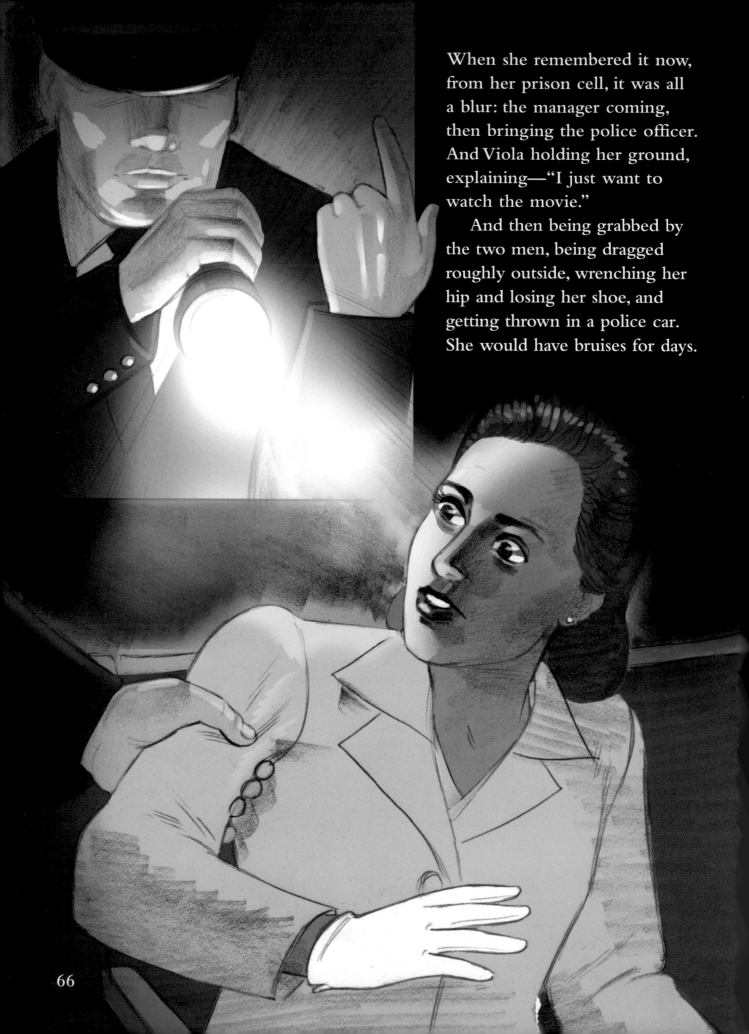

When she remembered it now, from her prison cell, it was all a blur: the manager coming, then bringing the police officer. And Viola holding her ground, explaining—"I just want to watch the movie."

And then being grabbed by the two men, being dragged roughly outside, wrenching her hip and losing her shoe, and getting thrown in a police car. She would have bruises for days.

Sitting there scared and alone, she didn't know what would happen next. But we do.

The next morning, Viola would be taken to court and given no chance to defend herself. She would be found guilty of not paying full price for her ticket, fined, and sent home.

When she got back to Halifax, she would do another brave thing. She would choose to appeal her case—which meant going back to court to try to clear her name.

She wasn't fighting just for herself—she was fighting for all black people, saying: We won't be treated like this anymore.

Sadly, Viola wouldn't win the case. And that would be hard.

But what she would accomplish would be so much bigger. Viola Desmond would start a wave that wouldn't stop. She inspired other people to fight and demand change.

And eventually, change would come.

In the future that she couldn't see,
Viola Desmond's name would be known
all across Canada, and she would be a hero.
Even though her fight is not yet won,
Viola's actions remind us of what one
person can do to fight for good:
Hold your ground, speak out for
what's right, and never give up.

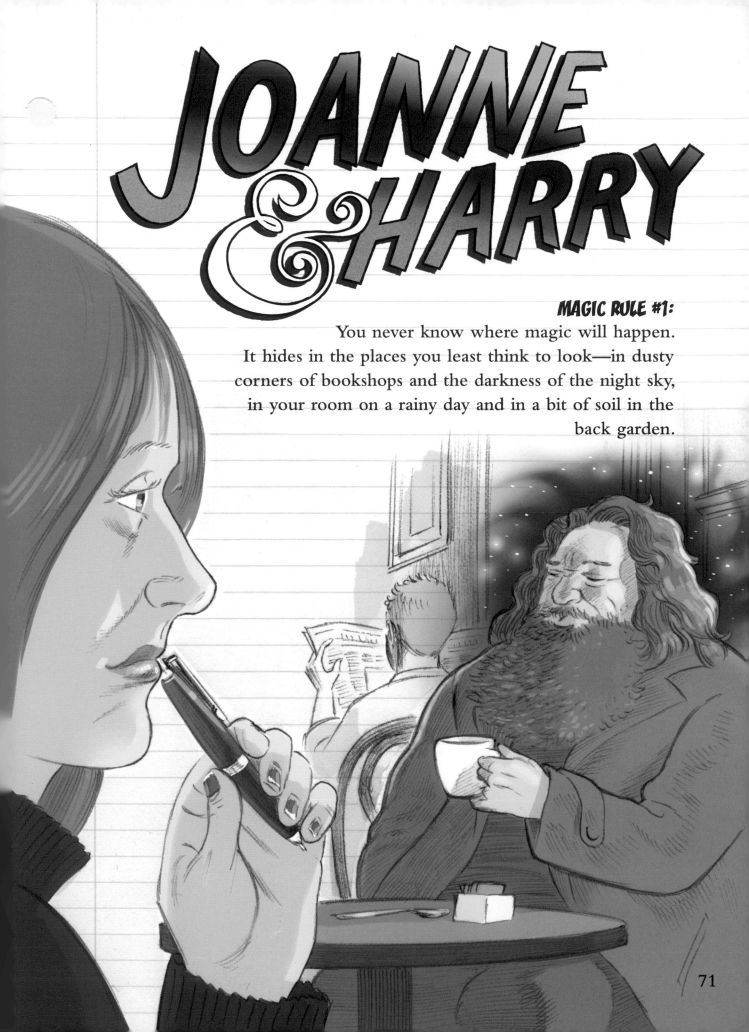

JOANNE & HARRY

MAGIC RULE #1:
You never know where magic will happen. It hides in the places you least think to look—in dusty corners of bookshops and the darkness of the night sky, in your room on a rainy day and in a bit of soil in the back garden.

If you'd walked into Nicolson's Café in Edinburgh, Scotland, in the early 1990s and seen Joanne Rowling frantically scribbling away, with her baby in a stroller by her side, you almost certainly would have thought nothing of it.

That's the way it's meant to be.

If you could see it coming,
it wouldn't be magic.

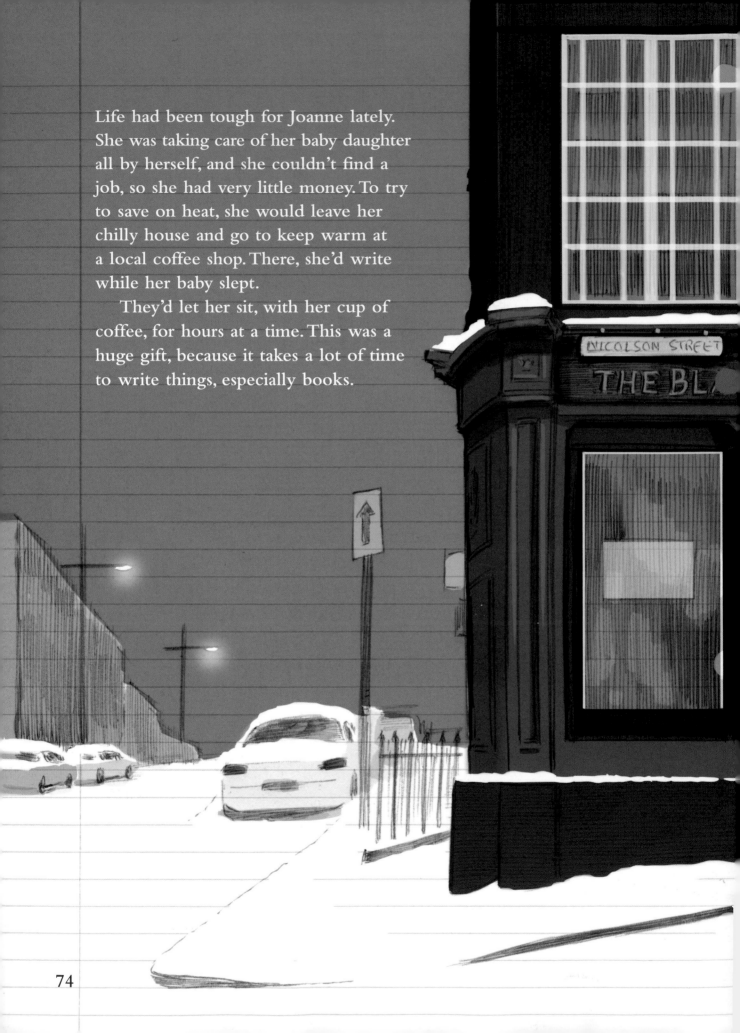

Life had been tough for Joanne lately. She was taking care of her baby daughter all by herself, and she couldn't find a job, so she had very little money. To try to save on heat, she would leave her chilly house and go to keep warm at a local coffee shop. There, she'd write while her baby slept.

They'd let her sit, with her cup of coffee, for hours at a time. This was a huge gift, because it takes a lot of time to write things, especially books.

74

But this café wasn't where the magic had started.
A very special idea had hopped into her head
before then, during a very long train ride.

MAGIC RULE #2: Always take a train if you get the chance—trains are special, and you will be surprised what you think of while you're whizzing down the tracks watching the trees and backyards and factories go by.

76

Joanne was on the train, and as she sat there looking out the window, a story came to her of a boy named Harry Potter who lives an unhappy, ordinary life, until one day he finds out who he really is: a wizard, with a famous past . . .

There would be a magical school where he would go to learn spells and potions, and there would be elves, and ghosts, and a horrible villain for Harry to defeat.

As time went on, in Nicolson's Café and elsewhere, the colorful, hilarious, spooky world of Harry Potter was growing in her mind. And so she wrote it all down on paper. It took her six years.

And then, once she had the first book written, she typed it all out on a typewriter, so that others could read it too.

Joanne wasn't sure anyone would like it. Certainly her friends didn't really seem to understand why she, a single mom on welfare, would spend her time doing something so . . . strange.

But she was hopeful, so she sent it out to some publishers, the people who make books, to see if they might be interested.

Twelve separate publishers said no, but she didn't give up.

MAGIC RULE #3: If you know there's magic in something but other people can't see it, that's probably because they're not looking hard enough. Keep trying and you'll find someone who can see it too.

Maybe it will be a friend or a teacher or someone you don't know yet. In Joanne's case, it was a man named Barry Cunningham at a company called Bloomsbury. He read the book and liked it, and he thought, *Let's give it a try.*

So they printed five hundred copies and sent
them out to stores.

82

MAGIC RULE #4: You can always find magic in a good book. And J.K. Rowling's *Harry Potter and the Philosopher's Stone* is a very good book indeed.* So many people read it that publishers had to print more and more copies. Hundreds, then thousands, and then millions.

Joanne Rowling wrote more Harry Potter books, seven in all, and they became the most popular book series ever. She never had to worry about having enough money to heat her house again, though she never forgot where she came from.

*You might know it as *Harry Potter and the Sorcerer's Stone*.

It's amazing to think it all started when she listened to that little magic voice inside her saying, *What if there were a boy wizard who didn't know he was special?*

She believed in herself, just as you should, even when things got tough. Because . . .

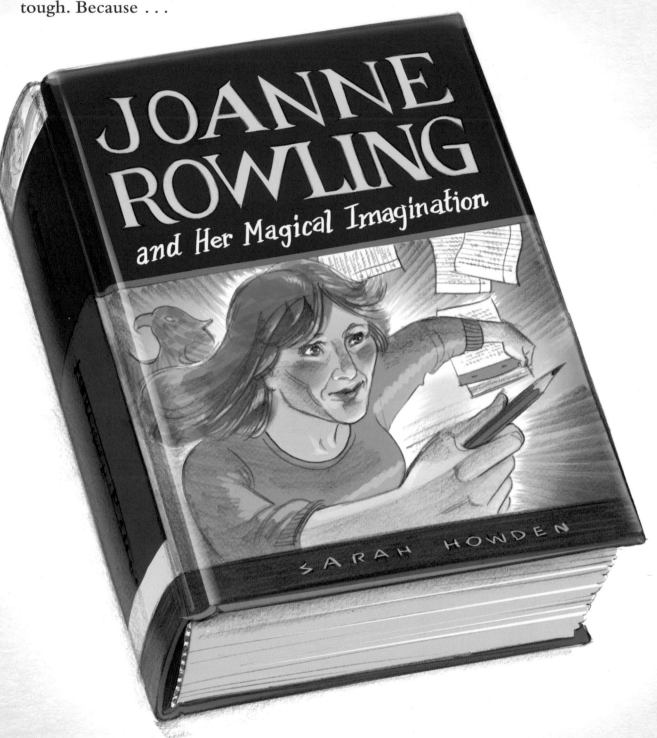

MAGIC RULE #5: You have a magic voice inside of you too. Listen to it, have faith in it, and you never know where it might lead.

HAYLEY WICKENHEISER,
HOCKEY LEGEND

Seven-year-old Hayley Wickenheiser is out on the ice rink in her backyard, late at night. She was up anyway, and she wants to get in more practice time. It doesn't matter that it's dark. She can feel the puck with her stick, hear where it's going.

Her dad comes barreling out the back door to find her there, her skates making snick-snick sounds on the lumpy ice.

"Hayley, what on earth? It's pitch black out here!" he says. But she can hear the smile in his voice. He doesn't really mind.

"I couldn't sleep," Hayley says with a shrug, before passing the puck to . . .

FLICK

Hayley at ten years old. She's been playing on boys' teams her whole childhood, but she doesn't mind. She's just as good, so most people don't seem to care. Although some parents tell her she should be playing ringette or doing figure skating.

Because she can't use the boys' change rooms, she changes in the back seat of her parents' car, in boiler rooms, any out-of-the-way place she can find. And sometimes she'll tuck her hair up under her helmet, so it isn't so obvious.

One day it'll be different, she thinks to herself.

"Good stickhandling," says her coach as Hayley deftly moves the puck back and forth, skating down the ice.

She nods and passes the puck to . . .

Hayley, five years later, getting off the bus with her midget AAA team. It was a long day, and everyone's ready to go home. But the coach calls her over and says they need to talk.

She can tell from his face it's not good news.

"Here's the thing, Hayley," he says quietly. "I just don't think you're the right fit for this team."

The shock takes her breath away. No way is this happening. She's been playing so well . . .

"To be honest, it just doesn't feel right, having a girl on a boys' team. I'm sorry."

Oh. So that's what it's about. She can't believe it.

Hayley can feel the tears forming behind her eyes, but she doesn't let them spill.

And the next morning, she's back at home, doing drills in the garage, pushing herself. She won't let this break her. Winding up with her stick, she slaps the puck over to . . .

Hayley on Team Canada. At fifteen, she's the youngest player ever to go to the Ice Hockey Women's World Championship, so she's nervous. Everyone keeps talking about how she's making history, but really she just wants to play well.

As they get ready for their gold-medal game against Team USA, she looks around at the faces of these players she admires so much: Manon Rhéaume in net, Danielle Goyette on the wing, Geraldine Heaney on defense. She feels so lucky to be learning from them.

But once the game starts, she has no time to think about any of that. Her only focus is the action on the ice. Hayley gets the puck, glances over her shoulder, and passes it to . . .

Hayley at the 2010 Vancouver Olympic Games. She's been to other Olympics before, won the gold medal twice, but this feels different. It's in her home country. And she's the team captain.

The semifinal game against Finland hadn't been easy, but they'd made it through. The Finnish goalie had seemed superhuman for a while, but Canada had just kept shooting.

FINAL SCORE: CANADA 5, FINLAND 0.

The next game is the big one: the gold-medal game against Team USA.

Team Canada may have won gold in the past two Olympics, but Team USA has won the last couple of world championships. Really, this game could go either way. They'll have to play their hearts out.

"We can do this!" Hayley calls to her team as they skate out onto the ice.

The crowd roars from the stands, and Hayley gets ready for the face-off.

Time seems to freeze as she waits for the referee. And then—she drops the puck. Hayley wins the face-off . . . and the game begins!

It's been a long journey getting here, but something tells her, deep down, they're going to win this game. In front of Canada.

In front of the whole world.

PRINCESS of the PEOPLE

Stevie was sick of being sick, and she was pretty sure no princess was going to help that.

She'd been in this hospital room for weeks, and she hated it. The nurses and doctors were nice and everything, but she just wanted to go home.

And now they were all in a tizzy about some visit from Princess Diana. Well, Stevie had other things on her mind.

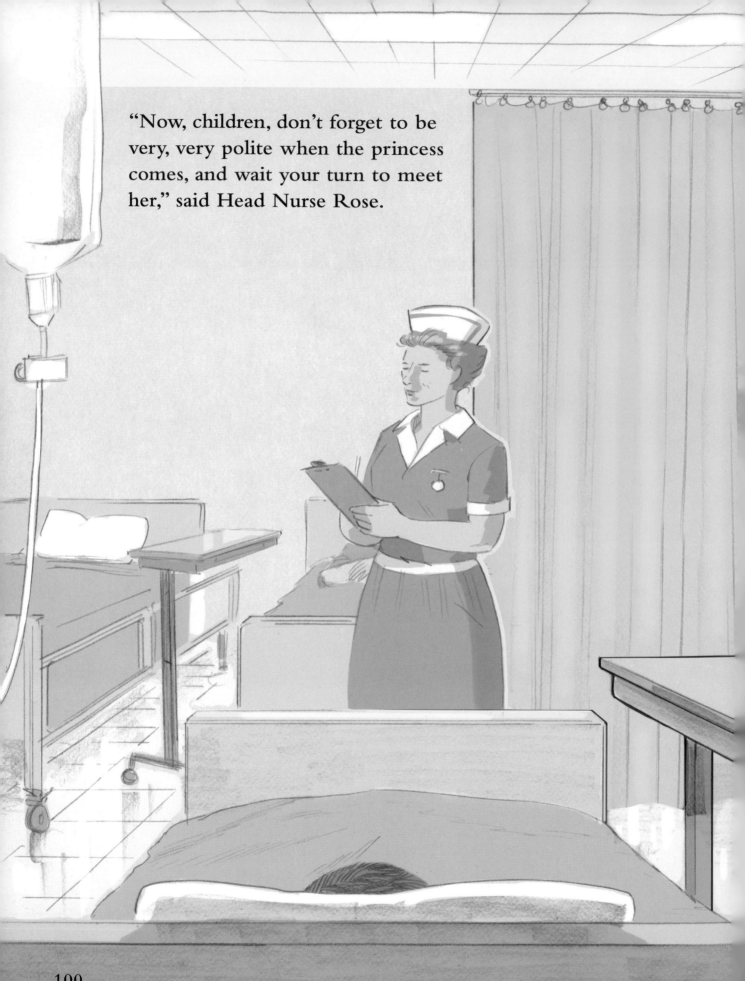

"Now, children, don't forget to be very, very polite when the princess comes, and wait your turn to meet her," said Head Nurse Rose.

"I'm not sure how much you all know about Princess Diana, but she's very special," added Nurse Gwen, her eyes sparkling. "She was a commoner, just like all of us, until she married Prince Charles. And now she's royalty! Going to fancy balls, wearing lovely gowns, meeting prime ministers and presidents—"

"And most important," Nurse Rose cut in, "as you'll see, she has shown herself to be a person of integrity." She wheeled in the TV and pressed play.

Stevie closed her eyes and got ready to nap. She didn't need to see any fancy gowns.

But as the announcer started talking, she opened her eyes again.

He said Princess Diana spent a lot of her time doing charity work. And not just easy stuff, like cutting ribbons at new hospitals in pretty dresses—this was real. Traveling to war-torn areas and lending a hand; visiting people in homeless shelters and hearing their stories; shaking hands with people who had AIDS and leprosy to show there was nothing to be afraid of. Still, Stevie wasn't going to get her hopes up. This princess may look like she cared, but it was probably all for show.

The next day, everyone was racing around like hamsters trying to get ready. There were banners and balloons and flowers everywhere.

Stevie's mom was there, and she was bubbling with excitement. She kept dabbing her eyes with a tissue and squeezing Stevie's hand. She even made Stevie wear a floppy green bow in her hair.

"Please, Mum, not the bow," Stevie pleaded, but at that very moment, Nurse Rose announced that Diana had arrived. And just like that, the princess was walking into the room.

There was something unreal about seeing her in person. Almost as if there was a glow around her, and a softness. She was taller than Stevie had thought, and her smile was even more dazzling.

"I hear she never wears hats when she visits kids," Stevie's mother whispered to her, "because she says 'you can't cuddle a child in a hat.'" She winked at Stevie.

Princess Diana wandered around the room slowly, making sure to talk to all the children and give them hugs or squeeze their shoulders. It was strange, but now that she was here, Stevie really wanted to meet her. She seemed so . . . nice.

108

And then suddenly, there she was, right
in front of Stevie's bed.

"Hello," said Princess Diana. She shook Stevie's mum's hand
and then her blue eyes settled on Stevie's. "And hello to you,"
she said, sitting down beside the bed and patting Stevie on
the arm.

"Hi. Thank you so much for coming," Stevie stammered.

The princess smiled warmly and said, "I love your little
bow." Stevie crinkled her nose but smiled anyway.

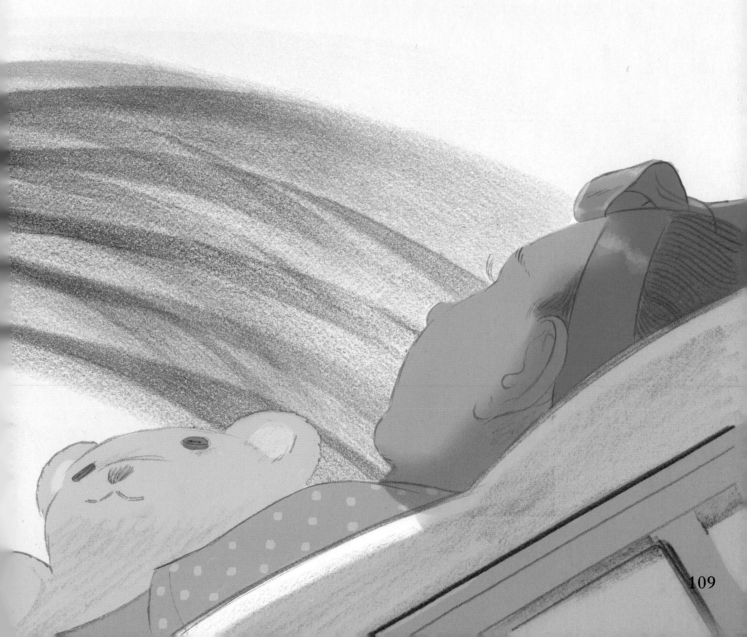

"I hope you're feeling okay. You know I think you're so brave, going through all this," Princess Diana said. Stevie felt a rush of pride wash through her, amazed that someone this important would think *she* was brave.

They talked a bit longer before the princess had to move on. As she left, Stevie felt her eyes get all watery.

The thing was, she'd been wrong. Princess Diana wasn't just a princess, she was a person, and maybe the most caring person Stevie had ever met.

"She said she wants to be the queen of people's hearts. Well, she is that," said her mum quietly.

Stevie nodded. "Yes, she is that." Then she added, "Horrible taste in bows, though."

She gave a giggle, and then her mum was giggling too, and suddenly they were both laughing—big belly laughs.

Stevie felt better than she had in ages. It turned out princesses weren't so bad after all.

DEEPIKA KURUP ASKS THE RIGHT QUESTIONS

In a way, Deepika Kurup was always a scientist, even as a little girl. Scientists ask questions and try to figure out how things work. They build things. And sometimes they solve problems.

Deepika was always asking questions. Why is the sun so hot? What makes plants grow? Why is candy so delicious?

And she liked to build. She helped build some bookshelves in her living room, gave her dad a hand putting together his new bicycle, and crafted windmills out of LEGO and K'NEX.

So maybe it's not a huge surprise that at fourteen, Deepika was named America's Top Young Scientist.

And it all started when she asked a question.

Every summer, Deepika's family would travel to India, where her parents were from, to visit her grandparents.

And every summer, Deepika's parents would remind her: Do NOT drink the water. If you drink it, they said, you can get very, very sick.

116

Over the years, Deepika got used to this rule. She knew it was just the way things were.

Until the summer before grade eight. As usual, her family traveled to India, and as usual, her parents told her the same thing: Do NOT drink the water.

But this time, Deepika found herself asking: What about the people who live here? What do they do?

When she looked around, she saw people lined up in the street filling buckets with water from a tap. She saw kids her own age drinking out of muddy puddles.

And Deepika realized:

They don't have a choice.

When she got home, she started researching, reading about how lots of people around the world didn't have clean water, and how many of them— including kids—wouldn't just get sick because of it. They would die. It seemed so unfair. Why should clean water be so easy to get in some places (like in New Hampshire, where she lived) but impossible to find in others?

People needed clean drinking water to live. It should be available to everyone.

Maybe I can help, Deepika thought.

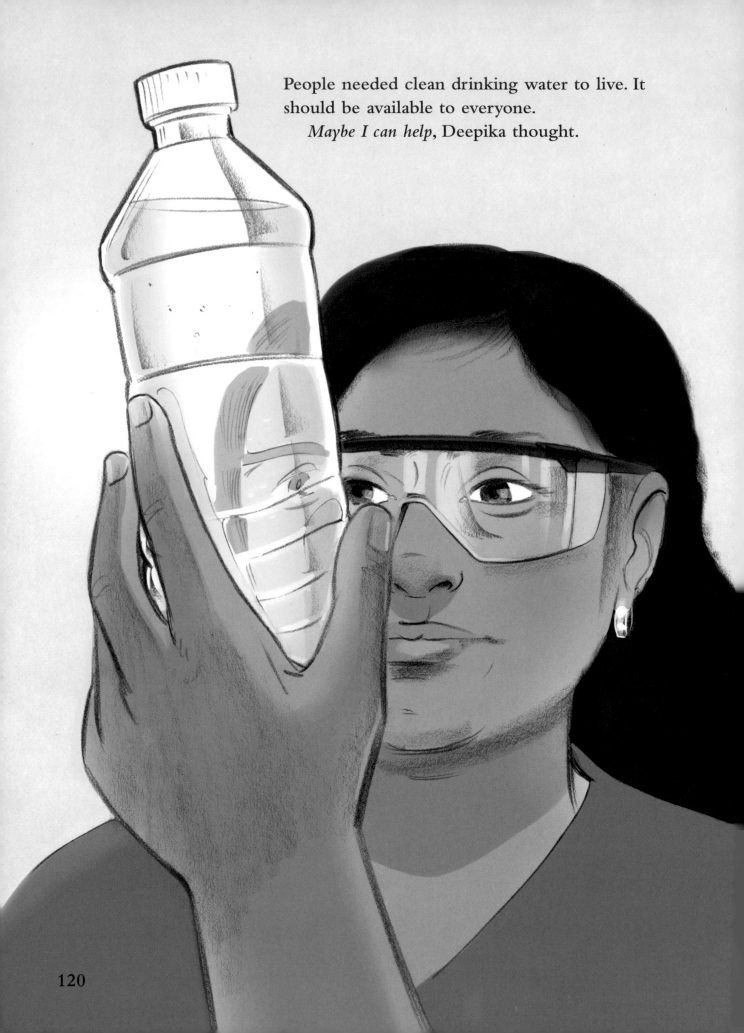

She started by asking another question: What are the best ways to make water safe to drink?

She found out that leaving water in a plastic bottle in strong sunlight worked . . . but that took six hours. And if the water was cloudy, which a lot of dirty water was, it could take up to *two days*. When you're thirsty, that's a long time to wait.

There were other ways to clean water too, but they were big, or heavy, or expensive, or complicated.

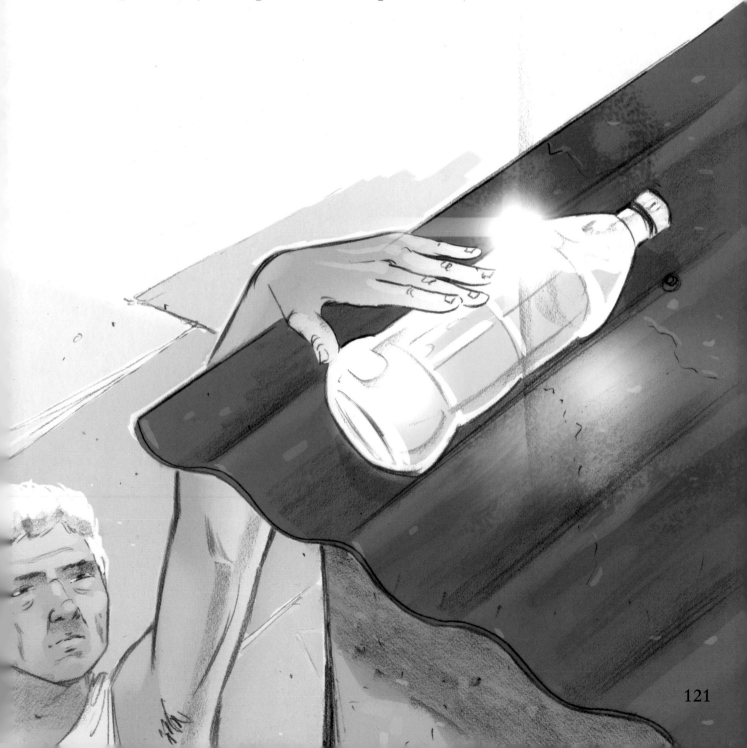

So Deepika made up her mind: She would make something better. Something that was light, and cheap, and fast, and easy. Something anyone, anywhere in the world, could use.

She set up a workshop in her family's garage and got started. Her goal was to create a filter that worked with sunlight to make dirty water clean.

She knew her project would take time. She'd need to build the filter, test it, see what went wrong, and then make it better. Over, and over, and over again.

For the next few months, Deepika experimented and perfected, until finally . . . it worked! She had designed a filter that could make a bottle of water safe to drink in only fifteen minutes.

THIS WAS BIG.

When she entered her filter into a national science fair, the judges thought so too—and she won! Her prize was $25,000 and that amazing title, America's Top Young Scientist.

Everyone was buzzing about Deepika's invention. She won many more awards and got to travel around and speak about her discovery.

She even met President Barack Obama!

Of course, Deepika still had one big question left: How can I get the filter to those who need it?

Her answer? By starting her own company. Through it, she could partner with others to turn one filter into thousands, which could be shipped around the world.

Soon, no matter where they live, people will be able to turn on their taps, fill a bottle, use Deepika's filter (with a dash of sunlight) . . . and drink down some clear, refreshing water—without worrying about it making them sick.

Her invention will save lives.

And all because she dared to look at a problem head-on. Instead of thinking it was too big to solve, she asked the most important question of all: How can I help?

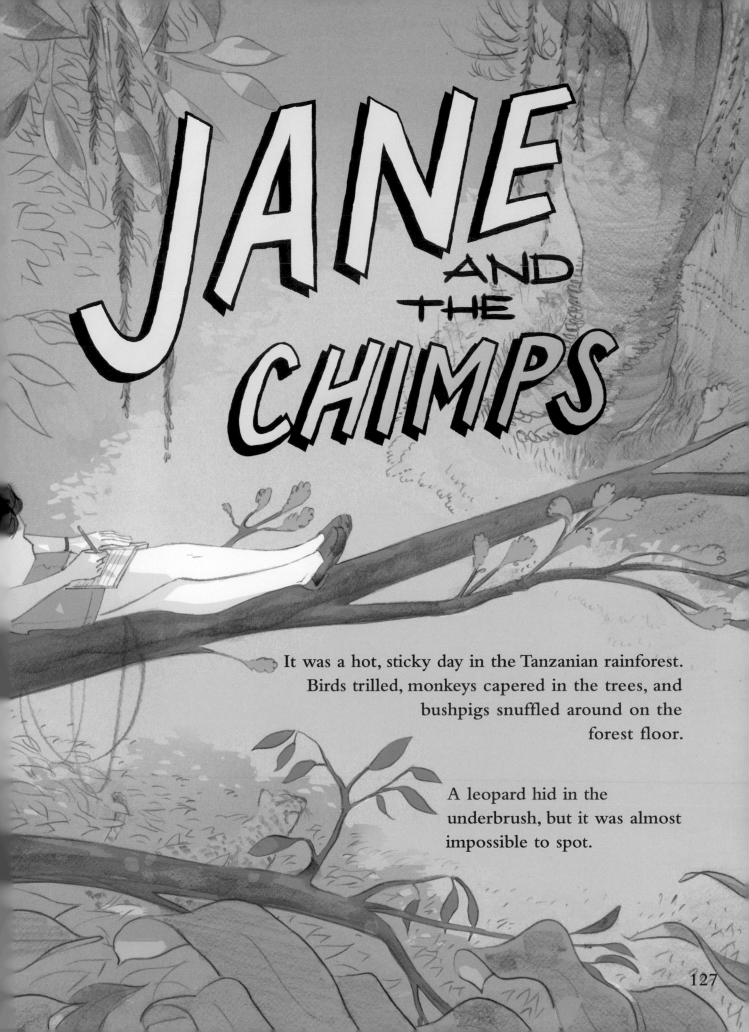

JANE
AND
THE
CHIMPS

It was a hot, sticky day in the Tanzanian rainforest. Birds trilled, monkeys capered in the trees, and bushpigs snuffled around on the forest floor.

A leopard hid in the underbrush, but it was almost impossible to spot.

What wasn't hard to spot, though, was the blonde
woman sitting up in the tree.

The group of chimpanzees knew she was watching them, this pale,
hairless ape, but they didn't know why. So they kept her at a safe
distance, running away whenever she tried to get near.

    The woman's name was Jane Goodall, and she was just now
wondering if this was all going to work out.

Her boss had sent her there to study wild chimpanzees and learn about their behavior. Even though she'd never studied animals before, and she hadn't even been to college yet, he'd taken a chance on her.

Deep down, Jane knew why: She was smart and brave, and she loved animals.

But how was she going to learn anything about these chimps when they wouldn't let her get close? Weeks had passed, and her little black cloud of worry was getting bigger and bigger. What if she failed?

131

A memory came floating back to her, from when she was four years old. She'd been staying at her grandmother's farm, and every day, Jane would help her grandma collect the eggs from the chicken coop.

But Jane wanted to know: How did hens lay eggs, anyway?

She'd decided the best way to find out would be to see for herself. So she climbed into one of the henhouses. In a flurry of feathers, the hen inside bolted out, squawking. But little Jane didn't give up. Instead, she settled into the corner and waited. Hours passed. Her legs cramped up and she almost fell asleep.

But eventually, a hen wandered in . . . and laid her egg. And Jane saw it. She was so happy!

133

Watching the chimpanzees was the same, Jane told herself.
She simply had to wait long enough.

Waiting wasn't easy,
but Jane was good at it.
And eventually, it paid off.

134

One day, while Jane was watching the chimp with the greyish-white whiskers on his chin—the one she'd named David Greybeard—she saw something incredible. He plucked a stick from the grass, stripped off its leaves, and stuck it down a termite hole. When he brought it out, it was covered in termites—which David nibbled off!

This might not seem that amazing at first. Especially the part about eating bugs. But what David showed Jane was that chimps can use tools. He'd made himself a fishing rod to fish for termites! No one knew animals could do that—they'd thought only humans were smart enough.

This was Jane's first big discovery.

David Greybeard helped her again, by being the first chimp brave enough to let her get closer . . . or actually, to get closer to her. He wandered into her campsite one day, tempted by some tasty palm nuts. And then he kept coming back. Once he even stole some of her bananas!

Jane started waiting for his visits, making sure to have bananas at the ready. Soon enough, David got used to having her around—he even took a banana right from her hand!

Jane knew then that David Greybeard was her friend. When he saw her in the forest, he would hoot his hello. And sometimes he would even join her up on the mountain, while she sat and did her research.

With David Greybeard's trust came the slow blossoming of trust from the other chimps, and over time Jane got to know them very well.

She learned that chimpanzees were a lot like people in other ways too—they had families and friends. They played, hugged and kissed, and felt fear and joy and sadness.

Now Jane Goodall is famous around the globe for the work she's done with chimpanzees—not just in showing us how they live, but in helping protect them and helping protect the planet.

It was worth all the time and the waiting to get to know these special creatures, to tell their stories, and to remind the world that animals and people might not be so different after all.

ZAHRA LARI, ICE PRINCESS

Zahra Lari was curled up on the couch, about to watch a movie. Outside her window, the heat of the desert was strong, even at dusk.

But when she pressed play, Zahra was swept away from her home in the United Arab Emirates to a much cooler place—an ice rink, where a teenage girl discovers her destiny as a figure skater. The movie was called *The Ice Princess*, and it changed Zahra's life.

141

Watching the skater glide and twirl on the ice, Zahra was transfixed. It looked so effortless. Well, except for the falling. Maybe she could take some lessons, just to see what it was like.

But Zahra knew in her heart she was hoping for more than that: She wanted to become a great figure skater. She wanted to be like the Ice Princess.

And so, at twelve years old, Zahra started skating lessons. Her parents thought, *This won't last long*. Figure skating in one of the hottest countries in the world? It seemed like a strange match.

But once Zahra began, she was hooked.

She spent more and more time at the rink, before and after school, trying to make up for lost time. Most figure skaters her age had started when they were three or four. She wasn't sure she could catch up.

Months went by, and she started feeling more sure of herself.

Even though sometimes her practice got interrupted by groups of schoolkids dropping in to skate, and even though the ice wasn't always clean or smooth, and even though spending so much time at the rink was giving her cold after cold after cold . . . she was improving. She was getting good.

So good that she started entering figure skating competitions, and people got to know her name. She thought, *I'm finally where I belong!*

But her father wasn't so sure.

He was a devout Muslim, and he was worried about whether it was proper for his daughter to be an athlete, to be performing in front of people like she was. Most women in the UAE didn't take part in sports at all, even for fun.

And he heard the gossip. People were talking about Zahra, shaking their heads and saying unkind things. Like: Should a good Muslim girl be devoting her life to figure skating?

Zahra didn't see the problem: She was still Muslim. She was still wearing her hijab (a headscarf that covers your head and neck). It didn't mean she couldn't skate.

But it troubled her father. Until he offered her a deal: She could keep skating, but she couldn't compete. If she really loved it, that would be enough.

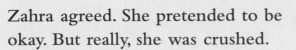

Zahra agreed. She pretended to be okay. But really, she was crushed.

She'd almost gotten there, to her dream. And now, she had to let it go.

Her father had done this only because he cared about her, she knew that. Even so, she felt sad, and lost.

Then one day, her father went with her to watch her friends skate in a competition. Zahra still liked to go, to see them perform, to cheer them on.

And when he looked over at her, clapping with all her might, he saw she had tears rolling down her cheeks.

That was when he realized how much she missed it. That she wasn't really okay. And he knew what he had to do.

"I'm sorry I made you stop," he told Zahra. "Please, follow your dreams. From now on, you can count on me. I'm behind you all the way."

Zahra was overjoyed, not just about being able to compete again, but that her father understood. Now no matter what other people said, she'd have her family on her side. And that was all she needed.

Zahra began training with more energy than ever.

This time, she thought, *nothing can stop me*.

It didn't take long before she was making history: At only seventeen, Zahra became the first-ever Emerati athlete to compete in figure skating internationally, and the first-ever figure skater to wear a hijab. And she's been competing ever since.

No matter where she goes from here, Zahra is proud of what she's done. She has opened the door for other Muslim athletes. She's gotten to live her dream.

And she doesn't mind at all when people call her "Ice Princess."

MICHELLE OBAMA, SUPERHERO

"Darlene, could you help with the knot-tying demonstration for Mrs. Obama?" Ms. Williams, our troop leader, asked.

Yes, *that* Mrs. Obama, the First Lady of the United States.

It wasn't a dream: Mrs. Obama had invited our Girl
Scout troop to camp out overnight on the White House
lawn, as part of her Let's Move! campaign—to get kids
active and outside, instead of inside watching TV,
like my brother David.

All the other Scouts seemed so excited. But I felt like
there was a hamster wheel in my stomach, spinning around
and around.

When Ms. Williams asked her question, the wheel spun
even faster.

"No, thank you," I said. I knew I couldn't do it. Not in
front of *her*.

Michelle Obama was so cool. Because of her, a chef came to my school and taught me and my friends how to cook a stir-fry that even David would eat. And when my dad lost his job, I got my school lunches for free, thanks to her.

My dad said she didn't have much money either, growing up. She used to live in a tiny house and share a room with her brother. I lived in an apartment and shared a bunkbed with David. So we were sort of the same.

But she could get up in front of hundreds of people and give speeches that blew them away. She was helping girls in other countries get a fair chance at going to school. She was one big reason why her husband, Barack Obama, got elected president. Plus, she'd met Elmo and Beyoncé.

On second thought, we weren't the same at all. **SHE WAS A SUPERHERO.**

When the day came and I stepped onto the South Lawn, I couldn't believe I'd be sleeping there that night. The grass was so green and lush, and the White House looked like a castle.

After setting up, we all gathered around the campfire. Our troop leader was leading a sing-along when Michelle Obama appeared. She looked so tall and regal in person. The hamster wheel inside me was going at super-speed. Some kids ran over and said hi, but I couldn't. No way.

She started talking to us, welcoming us there, and telling us how amazing it was that we liked to camp and have fun outside. She told us the White House grounds were actually a park and that we were making history by staying overnight there.

And then she told a story about how when she was little, she spent a lot of time being afraid. She said even though she got good grades, she never stopped worrying that she was going to fail.

She was afraid of getting an answer wrong in class, or failing a test, or looking like she didn't belong.

People, teachers even, sometimes made her feel she wasn't good enough. Because she was black, because she was a girl, because she came from a poor neighborhood.

And then she paused for a second and looked at all of
us, even at me, and she said, "I wish I hadn't been so
afraid. And I hope you all will try to fight your fears
and believe in yourselves."

164

"Because it's okay to make mistakes. And even if you do, you can always get back up and try again. Just do your best, and you can't go wrong."

It was funny, but as I'd been listening to Mrs. Obama, the hamster wheel seemed to slow down. I think I even started to feel . . . excited.

Afterward, I went over to Ms. Williams and asked, "Can I still help with that demonstration?"

She grinned and led the way.

When Mrs. Obama came over to our station, I was still nervous. My hands were shaking. But when she asked each of us for a high five, I did it! My hand was clammy, but I did it.

Then our group showed her how to tie a basic knot called a square knot.

I didn't get mine right until the second time. But Mrs. Obama didn't either. And that was okay. We had both tried our best.

Maybe we had a tiny bit in common after all.

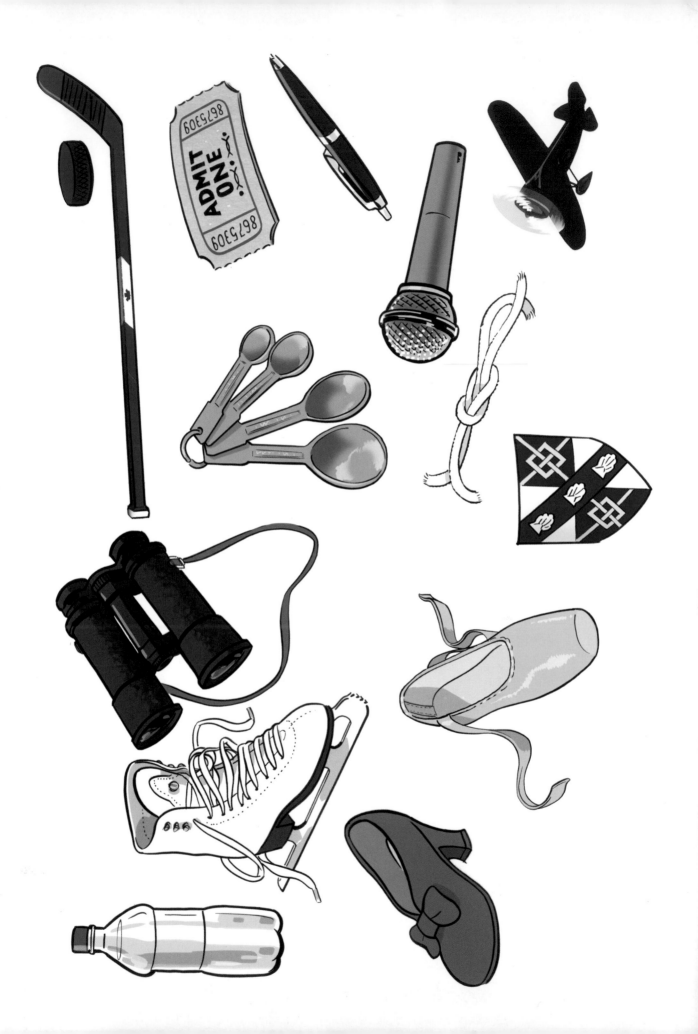